Morning on Solomons

JOHN "SONNY" ROBINSON

BELLE ISLE BOOKS
www.belleislebooks.com

Copyright © 2021 by John "Sonny" Robinson

No part of this book may be reproduced in any form or by any electronic or mechanical means, or the facilitation thereof, including information storage and retrieval systems, without permission in writing from the publisher, except in the case of brief quotations published in articles and reviews. Any educational institution wishing to photocopy part or all of the work for classroom use, or individual researchers who would like to obtain permission to reprint the work for educational purposes, should contact the publisher.

ISBN: 978-1-951565-22-0
LCCN: 2021901286

Cover and layout design by Michael Hardison
Production management by Haley Simpkiss

Printed in the United States of America

Published by
Belle Isle Books (an imprint of Brandylane Publishers, Inc.)
5 S. 1st Street
Richmond, Virginia 23219

BELLE ISLE BOOKS
www.belleislebooks.com

belleislebooks.com | brandylanepublishers.com

This book is dedicated to the memory of my father,
ELLIS W. ROBINSON,
a man with no formal education but with a big heart and a lot of country common sense; and to the other watermen on Solomons Island. Remembering back nearly eighty years sometimes distorts one's recollections, but brings forth many shining memories, which can be good, bad, funny, or serious.

CONTENTS

REMEMBERING *MISS LILLY* AND CAPTAIN WASH	1
A MOMENT NEVER TO FORGET	5
MY FAVORITE TOY	7
THE VICTORY GARDEN	9
A LESSON FOR MY GREAT-GRANDMOTHER	11
WAITING FOR THE BUY-BOAT	14
THE BIG FREEZE	17
ARTICLE FROM THE DECEMBER 14, 1949, EDITION OF THE *BALTIMORE SUN* NEWSPAPER	19
HARVESTING BLUE CRABS	24
MY DAD'S WISDOM	27
A WEEKEND SAVED	31
AN ISLAND TEENAGER'S SUMMER JOB	34
OUR FAMILY FOOD FIGHT	37
A WEEK IN THE PRINCIPAL'S OFFICE	39
THE CHESAPEAKE SKIPJACK	42
CODE OF THE WATERMEN	44
DANGER ON THE WATER	49
A BOAT WITHOUT A RUDDER	51
DON'T EAT THE SEAFOOD	54
A WATERMAN'S CHRISTMAS	56
A LIFETIME OF SERVICE	58
A Fireman's Prayer	59
A Fireman's Prayer II	60
About the Author	63

PREFACE

In this book are gathered short stories relating my recollections of true events from my early years. I was blessed to grow up in a small community located on Solomons Island in Calvert County, Maryland. However, at the time, knowledge of opportunities for a better life were all but nonexistent. There were times when young people in our position found the obstacles to our personal growth very hard to overcome, due to lack of sponsorship or encouragement from the older inhabitants of the island.

To begin with, I would like to offer a short introduction to the island as it was in my youth: a small piece of land shaped like a pipe stem, located near the mouth of the Patuxent River. The most unique feature of Solomons Island is the depth of the surrounding water. To the west of the island, strong winds and currents had carved a channel over two hundred feet deep. During World War II, the Navy used this area to submerge one or two submarines to protect them from a possible aerial attack. The deep-water entrance to the main harbor allowed a steamboat a weekly visit to dock and embark passengers and mail as it streamed between Baltimore and Virginia's Hampton Roads. The steamboat pier, as it was called, also provided dockage for off-season buy-boats as they unloaded their cargos of watermelon or lumber.

In addition to the steamboat and buy-boats, many private yachts also visited the island for short overnight stays, or to allow their owners to dine in one of the fine seafood restaurants along the shore or in town. The island was home to two wooden hotels: Recker's and Bowen's Inn, each with overnight dockage, nightly live music, and slot machines. Activities for younger children were limited to adventures on small sailboats, a sandy beach, and a movie theatre set over the water on wooden pilings.

REMEMBERING *MISS LILLY* AND CAPTAIN WASH

I remember him well: lean, and tough as nails. "Wash," as he was called, was a Chesapeake Bay waterman all his life. He was also my grandfather.

Captain Washington "Wash" Tilden Robinson was born in Annapolis, Maryland and moved to Solomons Island around 1900, where he raised nine children. During those times, making a living on the water was tough. Even though seafood was plentiful, prices were low. Harvesting oysters, fish, and crabs, when they were in season, made up the bulk of his livelihood. Oysters netted twenty-six cents a bushel; soft crabs sold for one cent each; fresh fish, two cents a pound. With so many mouths to feed, his family ate almost as much as he sold.

The waterfront property he rented had a small whitewash house with an attached woodshed, as well as a small wooden pier—most important for his prized possession: his boat, *Miss Lilly*. The johnny house was situated in a prudent spot twenty yards behind the main house. At night, the women used a slop jar, an option that was most appreciated during cold winters. The house itself was void of modern amenities, including running water; a pitcher pump, which had to be primed before each use, was attached to the small kitchen sink. In the center of the lone gathering room, or parlor, was a wood-burning stove surrounded by chairs of all makes and sizes. The stove had to be tended all night, limiting a good night's sleep to whichever boy whose turn it was to keep the embers lit. The house was drafty, and during cold, windy winter days, it was not unusual to see the curtains blowing out from the windowsills. The two small bedrooms upstairs had no heat, but homemade quilts, some collected and some sewed by the girls, were prized for their looks and warmth.

Luckily, next door to the property was a small railway that could haul one or two workboats at a time out of the salt water for maintenance. For a waterman, this ritual was necessary each year to clear barnacles, check for rotten wood, and apply a fresh coat of copper paint to the bottom of the hull of his boat. Captain Wash was a master at these tasks, and supplemented his income handily by working long hours to cut downtime for the boat owners, as lost time equaled lost income.

The Miss Lilly *with author on top*

All this work took a great deal of time, of course; so it was fortunate that there were four boys in the family to help with chores around the house. In most families of the day, boys followed in their father's footsteps in learning how to earn a living. This fact was never truer than in a waterman's family, in which the long hours and hard work often took their toll. Formal schooling was considered nonessential, as Captain Wash instilled in his sons his considerable knowledge of the best ways to take advantage of all the Chesapeake had to offer.

The four boys, including my father, Ellis Washington Robinson, followed their father to the sea. However, my father was also lucky enough to attend the one-room schoolhouse on Solomons for four years. During this short period of schooling, he learned to read and spell, and developed a fine ability for writing cursive. Later in life, as he moved away from working on the water, the schooling allowed him to hold employment with the Patuxent River Naval Air Station as foreman of the boat house.

Captain Wash, on the other hand, had never learned to read or write. When I was a teenager, it was my job to take my grandfather's seventeen-dollar social security check, marked with his "X," to the store each month and return with a six-pack, followed by a visit to the property owner to pay his seven-dollar monthly rental payment. This was a very valuable lesson for me, as it was my first real experience handling money.

I remember seeing my grandfather for the first time when I was five years old. At the time, my family lived in the Dundalk area of Baltimore, but we were visiting Solomons Island for the weekend. My father took me to the back shoreline, where my grandfather was in the process of building his own work boat, modeled after a log canoe. It didn't look like a canoe, but rather got its name from the rounded hull and pointed bow and stern. The boat looked huge to my young eyes. It measured about thirty feet in length and six feet wide, with twelve-inch gunnels built forward to aft for use as a platform for tonging oysters, as well as a small cabin to ward off cold winter winds. Any shipwright would have been proud to see the workmanship my grandfather put into his labor of love.

The next time I saw the boat, it was floating at his small pier, all painted and proudly sporting the name *Miss Lilly*, after my grandmother, Lillian Graves Robinson. In years to come, my family and I would spend many hours on the boat, working and playing, and sometimes just cruising the beautiful blue Patuxent River.

Captain Wash labored, as all watermen did in all types of weather, on his homemade boat for nearly forty years, and proudly catered to many of his children and grandchildren whenever a request was made to go fishing, pleasure cruising, or visiting family along the river. It was a sad day when he reached the age of seventy-seven and his four boys united to persuade him to retire from working on the water, for fear of the dangers inherent to working alone at his age. The last time I saw the *Miss Lilly*, she was at the end of a hemp rope being towed to a new home, like a proud workhorse that had served its master well and earned the right to retire with her builder and her Captain.

A MOMENT NEVER TO FORGET

In the early 1940s, the world was in turmoil, and events taking place around the globe touched everyone sooner or later. I remember one beautiful Sunday morning when my family was visiting my dad's parents on Solomons Island. Dad's three brothers, my uncles Claude, Ollie, and Elwood, were gathered on the side porch, taking turns cranking the handle on an old wooden ice-cream maker. I was five years old and excited for dessert after Grandmother's baked rockfish dinner. It was a special treat to eat at her house on Sunday, where we were treated to a large striped bass stuffed with homemade dressing, and to sliced potatoes cooked with the fish, with cranberry salad on the side.

As I stood anxiously, watching the family joking and happy, my grandmother slammed open the screen door from inside the kitchen and yelled, "Oh my god, the Japanese have bombed Pearl Harbor—we are going to war!"

The mood changed so quickly. I didn't fully understand what had happened. But there were four young men standing there, all in their twenties, and they understood all too well that their futures had suddenly changed.

No one knows the future for sure, but God surely must have been looking out for our family—none of my grandmother's boys went overseas to the fighting. My dad had a physical handicap, Uncle Elwood was already working at Patuxent Naval Air Station, Uncle Ollie was in the Coast Guard, and Uncle Claude worked in the naval mine warfare test center associated with the naval base. The biggest change that came to my family as a result of the war was that my dad relocated us back to Solomons from Baltimore and became chief of the naval base boathouse. In this position, he was responsible for the maintenance of PT boats and coastal patrol boats, key at that time for surveillance of the waters around the air station.

But that was a morning I will never forget.

Ellis W. Robinson (circa 1950)

MY FAVORITE TOY

Today, toys are everywhere. Certainly Walmart or Amazon can furnish a larger variety than any child can hope for. Not so when I was growing up.

During my first and second grades, my family lived in the Dundalk area outside of Baltimore, Maryland. Most of our other relatives lived on Solomons Island, and my mother and father made the ninety-mile drive every weekend Dad could get away. I looked forward to the visits, because I was allowed to explore the shoreline on my grandfather's property. When you are on an island, you never know what treasures may wash up from the sea, waiting to be salvaged.

Along this section of shoreline near my grandparents' house was a thicket of gall bushes, which served as a filter to trap whatever debris washed in with the wind and tide. This area became my playground, and often furnished the materials I needed to construct my favorite toy.

The main item I needed for this toy was a four-by-eight-inch slab of cork two inches thick, gleaned from an old, discarded life vest. You can't imagine how excited I got whenever I found an undamaged slab; it was a rare find, because cork was being phased out as a flotation material in life vests. The slab became the hull of my very own sailboat. A twig from one of the gall bushes, inserted into a small rectangular piece of cardboard, became a mast to support a tiny sail. Tin can lids served well as both the keel and the rudder, as they were easily inserted into the cork bottom.

It was a special day if I could find enough pieces to outfit two boats and hold an imaginary world racing championship. I never expected my boats to return to the shoreline. My greatest satisfaction was to watch as the wind blew them into the river and out of sight.

When I grew older, my fantasy of racing boats became a reality. I purchased a sixteen-foot inboard hydroplane that I named the *Miss Solomons,* and raced her up and down the East Coast in sanctioned regattas, including the Washington, DC Gold Cup and the Florida Orange Bowl in Tampa.

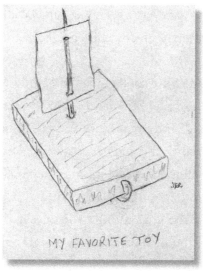

above: Sketch by author | below: Author's 145 cu in class hydroplane

THE VICTORY GARDEN

During the war years of the 1940s, food became scarce, and ration stamps were issued to most citizens. Many of the people who lived in the countryside were lucky enough to have a small plot of land on which to grow their own vegetables. These plots became known as Victory Gardens.

When I was eight years old, my family kept a small garden that helped to supplement our meals; but some of our neighbors did not or could not have one. My first paying job came about thanks to my small Red Ryder wagon. One of our neighbors had a very nice-sized garden, about fifty by two hundred feet, where they grew every vegetable I ever knew. He asked my mother if I would be interested in filling my wagon with his produce and selling it in our small community.

Saturday was my day to help my neighbor load the wagon, after which I walked up and down several streets, ringing a large bell my neighbor loaned me to get attention as I walked along. I knew everyone in the community, but I was surprised by how many ladies visited my wagon. Tomatoes were a big seller at one cent each, as well as spring onions at four cents a bundle and cucumbers and peppers at three cents. Some Saturdays I had to replenish my wagon before continuing on my route. Even though we had our own garden, my mother was a good customer. I was excited the first time my neighbor gave me seven cents pay.

My job only lasted two summers, as the war ended and food supplies became more plentiful. Many of our neighbors continued to grow their gardens after the war, as they realized the many benefits of keeping such a garden. My neighbors were happy when the rationing stopped, but they all felt that in some small way, their private gardens had helped the war effort. As for me, I was too young to know or understand my small part in history.

A LESSON FOR MY GREAT-GRANDMOTHER

Although Solomons is a small island, its early settlers were quite religious, building two churches on the island: the Methodist and Episcopal denominations, which are still serving the island's people today. A large Catholic church, located just off the island, dwarfs the two smaller buildings, reflecting the fact that it had the largest congregation.

The Methodist church, which I attended, had a small cemetery in its courtyard—a resting place for some of the settlement's early founders. The main chapel could seat about forty attendees, while a small wing on the back could hold about fifteen children for Sunday school. Neither section was ever full, except during funerals. Due to allocation of available space, three different Sunday school classes—one each for junior high students, high school students, and seniors—were all held in the main church area.

My great-grandmother, Nettie Jones, lived three houses down from us, in a small four-room house she rented for four dollars a month. The house had no running water or bathroom facilities. She was my babysitter whenever my parents left for an overnight trip. Every Sunday morning, rain or shine, she walked to church, and as she passed our house, she would escort me to and from Sunday school.

As the years passed, I progressed through the various Sunday school classes. During my second year in the high school class, our teacher moved off the island, and we were left with no class leader. On the following Sunday, I was requested to fill in until a senior leader could be located. I found that I enjoyed preparing for each lesson, and continued in my role until I graduated from high school.

One Sunday morning, we learned that the leader of the senior class was out sick—so when I was asked to meld the two classes into one and lead the Sunday school lessons for both the high school and senior classes, I couldn't say no. I was more nervous than I had ever been, leading my ninety-year-old great-grandmother into my interpretation of the material before us. I don't know if I was successful or not, but I thought my great-grandmother was very proud.

Solomons Methodist Church

Morning on Solomons

Sketch by author

WAITING FOR THE BUY-BOAT

Today, buy-boats are a thing of the past. Due to the decline of oysters in the Chesapeake Bay, most buy-boats were allowed to deteriorate and fill with water over the decades, sinking to the bottom of the harbors they once served.

Fortunately, several buy-boats have been restored to beautiful yacht like condition by history enthusiasts. This group of modern seamen proudly travel the Chesapeake Bay to relive a bygone era, graciously allowing visitors to board their boats to enjoy a sight like no other. Once aboard one of these reconditioned boats, a visitor must marvel at the effort required to transform a sunken abandon hull to this show piece. The average buy-boat is roughly forty feet long and ten to twelve feet wide. Diesel-driven, they travel at a slow cruising speed, which is just fine for relaxation. I have been very lucky to visit some of these boats, and as your mind takes you back to what they once were—everyday workboats—you better come to understand and appreciate their task.

The buy-boat was once the vehicle oystermen used to move their catches to market. It made several trips up and down the rivers every day, purchasing the day's catch from each waterman. The buy-boat captain paid two to three cents a bushel less than was paid at the packing house, but provided a valuable service that allowed the workers to stay on their locations and continue working in lieu of pulling anchor, motoring to the oyster-packing plant, and sitting in line to be unloaded. Some oystermen stayed onsite for one or even two weeks at a time. Each boat had a galley with a small wood stove to heat coffee and soup, and to make bread. This diet, along with raw oysters, was common fare for the oystermen.

It was not unusual for ice to form around the hull of an oysterman's boat at night, requiring him to complete an additional task each morning just to get working again. The work of an oysterman was hard: the pay was low, and oystering could only be done in the winter months, so it was always cold, making him thankful for the small wood burning stove in the cabin. Earning enough money to support a family meant being away from home a large part of the time. Handling eighteen- to twenty-four-foot tongs was back-breaking work, and even with a proper pair of gloves, callouses hardened the hands.

My grandfather, Captain Wash Robinson, had four sons who helped him support a family of eleven people. To earn additional money, he acquired a refitted work boat named the *Katie Collier*, which he used in part as a buy-boat. The Collier was put in service in 1931, but was only in use for four seasons, after which time it broke loose from a towboat, hit a sand bar, rolled over, and sank due to the weight of the oysters it held.

In 1938, Captain Wash began the special task of building a new workboat, which was to be named the *Miss Lilly*. As they got older, each of his four sons drifted away from the oyster business and went their separate ways. But my grandfather continued to oyster alone on his homemade boat until he was seventy-seven years old—though only on day trips.

Prior to renovation

The Katie Collier *after renovation*

THE BIG FREEZE

From January through February of 1948, the Chesapeake Bay area saw the lowest temperatures my family had ever witnessed. I was twelve years old and still in elementary school. Our school building was located half a mile away on the mainland, and all of us kids walked to and from school each day, rain, snow, or shine.

That year, the weather was exceptionally bad. The temperature dropped to a range of about sixteen to twenty degrees and stayed there for five weeks, freezing everything in sight. For most of us students, it was warmer at school than it was at home. My family had a small kerosene stove in the kitchen, but it didn't provide heat to any of the other three rooms. If you wanted to keep warm, it was necessary to rotate your body close to the stove, and even that barely helped. I kept the same clothes on for a week at a time. It was miserable.

The cold weather was far worse for the watermen. The waters surrounding Solomons Island froze solid, preventing any movement of workboats. The watermen could not work at their trade to support their families. In addition to creating a lack of work, the ice damaged boats and equipment, and more importantly, encased pier pilings—which were then raised out of the river bottom with the incoming tide, completely destroying some of the smaller piers.

The freezing ice continued to build until it completely encased the Chesapeake Bay and surrounding river waters. The center of the

Chesapeake Bay was frozen to a thickness of twelve inches, blocking all oceangoing cargo ships from reaching the Baltimore harbor. The Coast Guard relocated two icebreaker ships from farther north to open a channel from Virginia to Delaware, using the weight of their heavy steel hulls to crush through the ice.

The big freeze affected all inhabitants of the Bay area in one way or another. Some homes lost fresh water from individual home wells; others ran out of heating fuel. As the temperatures at last began to rise and the ice melted away, additional hard work began as the watermen made repairs so that they could once again have access to the water—and much-needed money.

ARTICLE FROM THE DECEMBER 14, 1949, EDITION OF THE *BALTIMORE SUN* NEWSPAPER

The following newspaper article depicts my middle school program's study of the growth of oysters over their lifespan. We spent four years recording the data, which was later turned over to the University of Maryland's biology department.

"Calvert County Boys Starting At Bottom"

by Audrey Bishop

Maryland's vanishing oyster may clap his bivalved shell when the news circulates to the bottom of the Chesapeake that 40 teen-age boys are putting their scientific knowledge into the fight to preserve him. Life, liberty, and the pursuit of happiness for the State's most valuable seafood resource are among the aims of members of the Students Marine Conservation Society at Calvert County High School near Prince Frederick.

The youths are observing how oysters live, feed, and reproduce by raising their own crop in areas of about two acres each at Broomes Island and Solomons. Through lectures and demonstrations by the school faculty and staff members of the Chesapeake Biological Laboratory they are learning the story of oyster depletion in Maryland and how applied farming, the rebuilding of bars, and law enforcement can help to restore and maintain higher levels of production. Similar projects are planned with fish, crabs, and terrapin, and the boys later may widen their study to include soil, forest, and game conservation.

Organized last year, the society is believed to be the only one of its kind in Maryland and perhaps in the nation. The group is limited to boys with access to the water and a boat. Its members live either on the Patuxent or the Chesapeake. They range in age from 12-year-old seventh grade students to high school seniors of 17.

Monthly Trips To Oyster Beds

Under the guidance of Miss Alice Evans, science instructor at their school, the junior conservationists hold discussion meetings in the classroom during activity periods on Mondays and Wednesdays. Field trips are made monthly to their oyster beds to which, through the co-operation of school authorities, the State's Department of Research and Education and the Department of Tidewater Fisheries, 4,000 bushels of seed oysters from Eastern Bay were transplanted last May.

At the time of planting the oysters were almost a year old and about an inch long. When they mature in 1950 or 1951 the youngsters will harvest and market the crop. Meanwhile, they are keeping records of the grown and general condition of the oysters and the cost of raising them.

The boys check the growth rate and the mortality of their crop by means of a test tray of 200 oysters in each bed. All tallies are based on these control groups so that the same oysters can be observed through maturity. A boat hook is used to raise the trays from the bottom. Each oyster's size is taken with calipers and recorded in millimeters. A "box," or dead oyster, is spotted quickly because its shell is open.

Conditions bearing on successful oyster production, such as the temperature and salinity of the water, are also observed, readings being taken with instruments.

On The Half Shell—For Study

The Solomons bed is just off the end of the pier at the Chesapeake Biological Laboratory, and on trips there the boys frequently conduct indoor experiments as well. Samples of diatoms, the one-celled plants on which oysters feed, are gathered with plankton nets and brought into the laboratory for examination under the microscope. Oysters on the half shell are specimens, not tidbits, to the young biologists who are learning oyster anatomy. They discover that an oyster may live for several hours after being shucked; they test its reaction to touch by jabbing the mantle or outer rim with a dissecting needle.

Under the direction of Dr. R. V. Truitt, director of the State Department of Research and Education at Solomons, the youngsters learn the life story of the oyster from fertilization of the egg to the marketing stage. With surprise they find out that the oyster is a free-swimming creature its first fifteen days or until it finds a hard substance to which to attach itself. Thus, the boys come to understand the importance of returning cultch to bay and river bottoms to catch young oysters and repopulate overexploited bars.

The club is learning first hand the difference between a natural oyster bar and a man-made one. The Broomes Island and Solomons beds serve as good examples. The latter has a hard rock bottom, which makes it a normal habitat for oysters. On the other hand, the Broomes Island bed with its soft bottom has never been suitable for natural oyster production. With their crop of 2,000 bushels of seed oysters and the planting of additional shell material on which future young can 'set,' the boys are endeavoring to develop it into a productive area.

Their Own Experimental Bags

Since the students' contact with the beds is limited to the monthly trips they make during school hours, Dr. Philip B. Whitford and G.

Francis Beaven, education assistant and oyster biologist, respectively, at the Solomons laboratory, have encouraged them in extracurricular projects in waters adjacent to their residences.

Trays of oysters have been made available to club members for regular measurement and observation at home. Several of the boys are determining the best spawning areas in near-by waters by placing wire bags full of shells at various points and marking the location by stakes. The bags are identified by tags, which are tin-can tops with perforated numbers. From time to time the youngsters lift the bags from the water to note the number of spat, or recently hatched oysters, which have attached themselves to the shells. The bag whose contents have accumulated the greatest amount of spat indicates the best spawning area. Temperature and salinity readings are included in the experiment to show the influence of these factors on breeding.

Some boys are recording the number of days worked by neighboring tongers, their average catch, and anticipated incomes. Others will visit the county clerk's office and get the number of licensed oystermen in 1880, compare this figure with today's smaller force.

Seeing Where Trouble Begins

As part of their conservation instruction, the club members last summer attended the "face-lifting" demonstration at the Thrasher farm in Frederick. While this was of general interest as an illustration of soil conservation, it held a special meaning for the young oystermen. Much of the damage to oyster crops, they were told, is caused by poor farming, which permits too rapid runoff of rainfall, which results in excessive silt and fresh water in rivers and bays. Silt clogs an oyster's gills and he is unable to feed properly. Enough of it can smother an entire bed. Fresh water is harmful since it lowers salinity.

Recently the group visited an oyster-packing house and watched its operation.

Author shown kneeling and measuring

The boys' own crop will not be ready for marketing for another year and a half. When the time for tonging is at hand, they will not need to be told how to do it. Many of these youngsters learned to manipulate a pair of tongs long before they ever used a pencil. Catching oysters is no task for them whatever. Their purpose is to master the problem of producing more oysters on the bottom and eventually greater income for their communities.

HARVESTING BLUE CRABS

Chesapeake Bay blue crabs are tricky to catch and difficult to handle, but the seafood meal that results from the catch is worth the effort. All crabbing tools are simple to assemble—I made my own as a teenager. Outside of wire crab pots, the next-best method of harvesting crabs is with a trotline, a method as old as Virginia and one that can be traced to the Jamestown settlers. The trotline consists of a heavy cord about one hundred yards long, and is weighted on each end with a lead sinker. The sinkers have an additional line attached to a buoy, which the crabber uses to locate the ends of the trotline. In the old days, the sinkers were marked with brightly colored pieces of cork, but today, empty plastic bottles are used.

A small boat with low risers and a broad, flat bottom serves the crabber as a base of operations. A roller bar—sometimes nothing more than a small piece of pipe fastened over a long nail—is used to guide the trotline along the side of the boat. Wooden tubs are used to contain the crabs after they are caught, and a notched wooden stick is kept handy for measuring, to ensure that undersized crabs are returned to the water. Finally, a most important tool for the crabber is a short-handled dip net, which has a wire basket about ten inches deep and twelve inches in diameter.

The bait that crabs prefer most is salted eel. Most crabbers use eel pots tied under their piers to catch the eels at night. The eels are cut

Blue crab painting by author

into two-inch lengths, washed, and covered in a salty brine mixture. The bait can be retained in this manner for up to one year if necessary.

To prepare to catch the crabs, the crabber skillfully attaches the bait to the trotline by a series of square knots every three feet along its length. The trotline is then coiled into a shallow tub or box from which it can easily be removed and set up by the crabber. Replacing the bait is a smelly task that must be completed at the end of each day, in preparation for early setup the following day.

An experienced crabber leaves home as the first rays of sunlight reflect in the morning sky. After years of crabbing in different locations, he knows to set his trotline across the mouth of an inlet. The crabber starts at one end of the line, pulling up the sinker by the attached buoy and inserting the line over the roller. The boat moves slowly along the anchored line and gently raises the line, bait, and crabs to the surface and the waiting dip net. The crabber's efforts are rewarded as the crabs appear on the baited line, and his cramped muscles strain to dip over and over.

People living on the East Coast have come to know the Chesapeake Bay blue crab as the king of the crustaceans. Most fine restaurants have several crab dishes on their menu. I prefer crab cakes, but I consider myself a connoisseur of any seafood dish containing the delicacy. Maybe it's the scene painted in my mind of the lone trotline crabber sitting in his small skiff, net in hand, as I once did, that brings me to this meal time and time again.

MY DAD'S WISDOM

It's October 1948. I am twelve years old. Tomorrow is Saturday, and I'm so excited I can hardly sleep, because my dad has promised to take me with him to work on the water.

I live on Solomons Island, a small pipe-shaped island at the mouth of the Patuxent River where it empties into the majestic Chesapeake Bay. Working on the water to earn a living is a way of life here. My grandfathers, "Wash" Robinson (Paw-paw) and "Piedmont" Jones (Poppie), both have their captain's licenses and earn their living from these waters. Paw-paw harvests oysters during the winter season, which usually lasts from October until mid-May. During the summer, he works as a shipwright. Poppie captains a fishing party boat, owned by a local businessman. I hear people say he's good at what he does, but Dad says he's lazy.

My dad, "EL" to locals, also spent his share of days working on the water when he lived at home, but not anymore. Now he works for the government as foreman of the boathouse at the Patuxent River Naval Air Station. It's his job to maintain the security patrol boats in ready condition so they can respond to any emergency situation that may occur during flight training. Dad only works on the water on his days off, to make extra spending money for the family. He says the price being paid for oysters is up, and we may get thirty cents a bushel tomorrow. With any luck, we'll board about two bushels an hour, and since we

Piedmont Jones

plan to work for four hours, we should net about two dollars and forty cents for our day's work.

I'm just hoping to earn enough money to go to the movies. It's hard to earn spending money as a young boy on the island in winter.

I hate to get up early, but all work on the water starts early. Dad is patient and takes my reluctance to rise in stride. The morning weather is menacing, the sky dull gray and overcast. Winds are twenty-five knots from the northeast, with the thermometer showing twenty-seven degrees. It is not your typical late October day.

As he does most Saturdays, Dad has arranged to borrow Paw-paw's boat, a V-bottom log canoe he hand-built. Today, I say a prayer thanking the Lord for Paw-paw's wisdom in adding a small cabin to the bow.

As we make our way out into the river, the salt spray driven by the wind soon engulfs the small boat, as if a spring thunderstorm has suddenly descended upon us. Dad uses the windshield wipers so he can see to maintain our bearing.

We do not go far into the river. Dad, wise in the ways of the water, anchors in an oasis of near-calm water close to shore. I feel better now, more awake; and some of the excitement has returned by the time he makes fast the anchor.

Dad uses an eighteen-foot-long pair of tongs to rake the oysters from the river bottom while maintaining his balance on the bobbing fantail. He handles the tongs with ease after years of working at this trade. He dumps the contents of the tongs on the culling board, a wide tray set across the boat, resting on the gunnels. The tray has open ends to allow the culler to sort the good oysters from the empty shells and undersized oysters. Normally, Dad handles both tasks, first filling the culling board and then culling out the good oysters. Today, he has a helper, which should allow us to harvest more oysters in less time.

EL is a small man, five feet five inches tall and about 118 pounds. His muscles are like steel bands from years of working on the water. He handles the tongs deftly and keeps the culling board piled high with a mixture of debris from the river bottom. Working the tongs is laborious, but the exertion helps offset the stinging cold and damp wind as it whips in gusts across the water.

As for me, I am dressed for the Arctic. This morning, I donned two pairs of pants, two pairs of socks, and two sweatshirts, all of which are covered by rubber boots, a long rubberized apron, and thick rubber gloves, and topped with a woolen stocking cap. I work as fast as I can, accumulating the keeper oysters in a haphazard pile around my feet while returning the unwanted residue to the river's angry surface on the opposite side of the boat. I have no time to watch the empty shells, small oysters, and other debris slip beneath the surface of the murky water and fade out of sight.

Standing there with oysters piled up to my knees, my rubber glove frozen in a knurled upturned position and every muscle in my young body aching, I suddenly understand why my dad no longer seeks to make his living on the water. I am tired. I am cold. At this moment, the movies seem much less important.

A long four hours later, we're waiting in line behind several other boats to unload our day's catch at Lore's packing plant. Dad shovels each measured wire basket level with the top. I know that this is the way of determining the value of the oysters. We only have five bushels, but Dad says that's okay due to the weather. We make a dollar and fifty cents for our morning's work.

I didn't know at the time what my dad was thinking when he chose to take me with him that morning, but years later, I came to the conclusion that he was a very smart man. Standing in that boat, I realized that I didn't know what I wanted to do or be when I grew up, but there had to be a better way to earn a living.

A WEEKEND SAVED

A waterman's boat is first and foremost a workboat, and for that reason it must be maintained in the best condition possible. The waterman's livelihood depends on the reliability of his equipment. Most all watermen are self-employed. No one encourages them to rise from a warm, comfortable bed before daybreak and head out to spend a day on the water, in good weather or bad, for an undetermined result at the end of the day's effort: some days, the fish just aren't biting, the crabs are scarce, or the oysters are mostly empty shells.

My father was considered one of the best, if not the best, at improvising repairs on Solomons Island boats. Workboats always took priority over pleasure boats. This work was not his primary job, so he could pick and choose which projects he wanted to take on based on his other activities, but he never turned down a waterman in need.

Located, as we were, sixty miles from the closest marine supply store, it was never easy to obtain major replacement parts in a timely manner. Most often, getting the replacement parts was just the beginning—additional downtime was required to make the repairs. But in the case of fishing parties, many trips were booked weeks ahead, and with a short season, missed bookings could ruin a fisherman's budget.

Case in point: one Saturday during our evening meal, my family's phone rang. It was Captain Langley, a fishing party captain fresh in from a day on the Bay, and he was having engine trouble. My father and I arrived at his boat to find a two-inch crack in the side of the engine block, a fatal problem that would have caused the engine to overheat. Normally, this type of repair required a minimum of four days for delivery of a replacement short block, so called because the attachments thereto were removed from the damaged block and transferred to the new one. This type of repair increased downtime, but ultimately saved money. However, Captain Langley's greatest concern was not the money, but the fact that he was booked for a Sunday morning and evening trip the next day.

My dad studied the problem, gave thought to the captain's situation, and proposed a temporary fix. He then sent me home to our very cluttered garage for a small four-inch square piece of sheet lead, an electric drill, and a tool and die kit.

An engine compartment on a fishing boat is very tight. Sitting cross-legged, Dad then carefully fitted the lead patch over the crack and drilled holes every inch around the perimeter of the crack. He then

Boats at Robinson's marina

threaded each hole to accommodate a small bolt, coated one side of the lead patch with a high-temperature gasket material called Permatex, and bolted it in place. It was after midnight when he turned to the distraught captain and told him that his fishing parties could go out as scheduled later that day, but he could not guarantee how long the patch would hold.

Captain Langley completed the fishing season before final repairs were made, and once again I observed a remarkable job well done and a captain's livelihood maintained, thanks to my dad's ability to improvise.

AN ISLAND TEENAGER'S SUMMER JOB

Growing up on a small island may seem to most people an idyllic, laid-back childhood. In many ways, it was. But living on an island comes with its own set of unique situations, as I was to find out. For instance, being in a very rural location, there was no plumbing or contractor service available to help with construction on small jobs.

Inhabitants of cities or large towns often take for granted many of life's everyday amenities. The one most important amenity I grew up without was indoor plumbing. We could not turn on a spigot and get hot water. Instead, you filled a kettle, placed it on the stove, and waited. This may seem a simple solution—unless you were in a hurry, such as when I was running late to catch the bus for school. But the lack of hot water paled in comparison to trekking outside to the john on a cold winter morning, sometimes through several inches of snow, not to mention the cold sheets of the Montgomery Ward catalog always present for use as necessary.

It was a total surprise, then, when in 1950 my father told me he was going to take part of my small bedroom to add a bathroom in the house, including a hot water tank. I was fourteen years old and couldn't believe we were going to have a bathtub with hot and cold running water.

There was no such thing as a local contractor, and even if there had been, we could not have afforded to hire one to do the work. The first thing my father did, with the help of his three brothers, was add a six-foot extension to the back of the house. This addition added a small screened-in back porch to the opposite side of the house from my bedroom, and extended my bedroom to make space for the new bathroom in the center of the house.

Little did I realize how much work would be involved for me to do. My being out of school for the summer worked well for my father's plan. My first task was to dig a footing trench across the rear of the house, following a string line Dad had set up for me to follow. While my father and his brothers worked on the subflooring and new walls, I was introduced to something called a septic tank.

First, I had to dig a round hole four feet in diameter and ten feet deep, and hope I didn't hit water. When you are five foot eight, a ten-foot-deep hole can be very scary, so Mother was always on watch. Dad took over as the depth increased, and I pulled each pail of dirt out with a homemade winch.

With the hole completed, the bottom two feet was filled with oyster shells lugged from Lore's oyster packing plant by wheelbarrow. Next, a fifty-gallon steel drum, which my father had procured somewhere and cut the top and bottom out of with a cold chisel and hammer, was lowered into the hole. Once in place, the outside of the drum was also packed with oyster shells. This drum was followed with a second drum with only the bottom cut out and a four-inch-diameter hole cut just under the top edge to accommodate the drainpipe from the house. This drum was also packed to the top around the outside with shells and covered to ground level with fill dirt. Our new bathroom was now ready for use.

My job still was not finished, though. Next came the removal of the johnny house and the filling of the space beneath. The hole was easily filled with the excess dirt from the new hole, some thirty feet away. It was not the summer I had looked forward to, but with school set to start the day after we finished, I went to bed that night looking forward to the many benefits of our labor.

OUR FAMILY FOOD FIGHT

Selections for island dinner tables were normally restricted to some type of seafood, and mothers worked hard to vary how food was prepared and served to their families. My mothers' favorite Sunday feast started with a fresh three-to-four-pound striped bass, which was then stuffed with homemade dressing complete with parsley, small potatoes, and sliced onion, all baked slowly until mouthwateringly tender. Homemade bread pudding completed the meal.

A more normal daily meal consisted of what today is called a pot pie. To make this, my mother would first make dough from flour, a dash of salt, yeast, and water, and roll it out flat before pressing it into a baking pan. Next, the pan was filled with a variety of meat, whatever happened to be available. It could be chicken, oysters, crab, fish, or ground beef, along with potatoes, sliced onion, and water. The top of the pan was then crisscrossed with dough strips and replaced in the oven until the dough was golden-brown. There was sometimes a treat for me, as Mother would gather the leftover dough into a ball and place it in the oven with dinner, after which a light coat of sugar was added to the dough, and it became my dessert.

One of my father's favorite meals consisted of soft-shell clams cooked in heavy stew. After stripping the clams from their paper-thin shells one Saturday, Mother prepared this meal for dinner; however, I do not like clams, and stated that I would not eat dinner. That statement started a bad discussion: Mother said I did not have to eat the stew, and my dad said that yes, I did. It was the first time I ever heard my parents have a verbal disagreement concerning me.

I did eat a little of the stew, but not the clams. I was sorry afterward, but it saved me from finding the bowl still at my place the next morning. Later in life, I had occasion to realize soft-shell clams really were quite good. Too little, too late.

A WEEK IN THE PRINCIPAL'S OFFICE

Growing up on a small island has many advantages, including ample opportunity to learn self-reliance, how to read the weather signs, and how to get along with your neighbors. However, not much thought is given to lifetime achievement. In the early 1950s, television was just coming into its own, but not many families on the island could afford one or understand why having a set was important. There were no hourly news flashes, commercials, or sports programs to guide a young mind one way or another when it came to a future lifestyle. It was no wonder, then, that most boys followed their fathers and grandfathers into a career working on the water.

I had none of the personal attributes required for such a future. I hated to get up early in the morning, and I wasn't a strong muscular person; nor did I fully understand the effort required to maintain the various equipment necessary for day-to-day work on the water. However, because of my background, my curriculum up to junior high was limited to the basic program, which did not include any precollege or advanced studies. It wasn't until I started high school, twenty-five miles away off the island, that a guidance counselor helped me look into what higher education programs might be available at a very low cost. My family had no money to support a college education, so I was doubtful that we would be able to find anything. However, it was during this time that the counselor located a small catalog from a trade school in Newport News, Virginia. The school appeared to fulfill my needs, with a work-study program available to help with finances. There was one big catch; I had to qualify by passing subjects not available in my present curriculum. I had missed the boat to attend the required courses with my classmates and was already a year behind, so now it was up to me to catch up as best I could. The required subjects started in the ninth grade, and at this point I was told it was too late this year to change my curriculum. Who cared about a young waterman's son anyhow?

Which brings me to the start of my scheduled tenth-grade classes. Initially, I was slated for the same minimal curriculum I had followed in previous years, but I would have none of it. On the first day of school, I went to the principal's office and refused to attend my scheduled classes. I was told it was too late and I could not change curriculums. The second, third, and fourth days were the same. I did not inform my parents about my actions; I did not think they would understand, and I wasn't sure about what I was doing.

On Friday of that week, several of my teachers met with the principal, Mr. Holland, and were asked their opinion as to my ability to double my workload in an effort to catch up. The key teacher involved was the math teacher, Mr. Smitz, a very fine educator who in fact had previously been a college professor. Several college professors had been sent to our high school due to lack of work in the colleges at the time.

Monday morning, I started my new course of study, which began with ninth-grade algebra and ended with tenth-grade plane geometry. Thanks to the help of faculty members and fellow students, I achieved my goal, earning enough credits to apply not only to Newport News, but also to Patuxent Naval Air Station.

I was accepted at both programs, and made the tough decision to leave home and attend the apprentice school in Newport News, Virginia. I did not fully understand the apprentice program, nor what a boilermaker was; but now I was training to be one. All work done by a boilermaker involves forming and fabricating heavy steel plating, much of which is accomplished while the steel is white-hot out of the furnace. I had worked hard in high school to qualify for this?

My first day on the job, I was sent to welding school to become a certified Navy welder, a requirement for all boilermakers. I was a long way from home, and very homesick, but I was proud the first time I returned home sporting my new school jacket. I was voted class president my first year, got along well with my classmates, and looked back fondly on my five days in the principal's office and how they had gotten me where I was.

Five years later, I was still class president, and spoke at our graduation ceremony. I graduated as a nuclear piping designer and was assigned to the design team on the first nuclear-powered aircraft carrier, the Enterprise. We were told it was necessary that we have a confidential clearance to work in this program, and filled out many forms; but the intensity of the checks did not become totally clear until the next time I visited home and Dad wanted to know what I had done to bring the FBI around questioning our neighbors.

I spent the next forty years working for the shipyard in various management positions—all because my schoolteachers believed in a young island boy's dream.

THE CHESAPEAKE SKIPJACK

To prevent overharvesting of oysters, powerboats were not allowed, by law, to be used for dredging. Therefore, the skipjack was a workhorse for crews dredging oysters from deep in the Bay, It was fast under sail and highly maneuverable, perfect for dredging oysters while cutting through the Bay's sometimes three-to-four-foot swells.

The only skipjacks on the Bay today have been restored and are mainly used for pleasure. However, I have recently seen a very competitive skipjack race in Maryland waters. Designed and built in America, this small sailboat had a clipper stern, a broad transom, a V-shaped bottom, and a single mast. The skipjack's one big drawback involved docking and undocking while in harbor, which generally could not be accomplished under sail. The solution to this issue was to use a pusher boat, a small but well-built skiff with a gasoline engine mounted inside and stowed across the transom on two davits. This arrangement allowed the skiff to be raised and lowered as needed, as well as to keep it out of the work area while at sea. Generally, the captain moored his boat overnight in his home port after unloading the day's catch at the oyster-packing plant. However, some boats ended the day by docking overnight in neighboring harbors, using open space not normally in use during cold winter months. On such nights, the crew stayed on board, working to repair damage incurred during their workday or just resting.

Early in the morning during winters, when the harbors are slick and calm and sometimes even coated with a thin layer of ice, the pusher boat was made that much more important. However, as with any gasoline engine, there is always a risk of mechanical failure, especially when it is subjected to salt water.

One evening, while our family was making do with a small dinner, the phone rang. My father answered it and announced that a visiting skipjack crew was having trouble with their pusher boat's engine. Dad said I could go along with him, as I sometimes did, and that the problem might be minor and not take long to repair.

When we arrived, we could see right away that the engine was not well maintained, and that it would take us some time to determine the course of action we would need to take to repair it. After two hours, my father sent me walking home, worried that the time spent trying to restart the engine would eat into my study time for school.

It was almost twelve o'clock when Dad returned home, having completed the repairs. He brought with him a half-bushel of oysters and a large four-pound striped bass, his pay for five hours of knowledgeable hard work. We were glad to have extra food for another week, or until the phone rang again.

CODE OF THE WATERMEN

When a young person first leaves home, it can be a traumatic event in any family's life. However, when that home and family are united with the sea, the lure of the sea never leaves. So it was, and is, with me.

While attending the Newport News Shipyard Apprentice School in Virginia, I proudly purchased my first used car so that I could make the 180-mile round trip home to Solomons Island every chance I got. It was during one of these weekend visits that my dad decided he wanted to take a break from work and spend the day together fishing.

My father owned two boats—a small cabin cruiser; and his favorite, a converted speedboat. The speedboat had once been used during prohibition as a whiskey runner smuggling whiskey across the Great Lakes to Canada. This boat was reminiscent of a modern cigarette boat—eighteen feet long and five feet wide, with a double door hatch to the engine similar to the very popular Chris-Craft. Unfortunately, the hull below the waterline was covered with a thin layer of copper sheeting for protection from the lake ice. The sheeting added weight and slowed the boat somewhat, but could not be removed due to the poor condition of the wood hull underneath.

The unnamed boat was so unique that most all the local watermen recognized it, but cared less that it was the fastest inboard on

Modified speed boat

the river. The boat had been stripped of most luxuries, including windshield, padded seats, navigation equipment, and ship-to-shore communication. My dad used it as transportation to and from his job at the Patuxent (PAX) River Naval Air Station Boathouse across the river, and occasionally for fishing on the weekends.

On this October Saturday in 1956, neither of us thought much about needing anything extra on board, except a container for the striped bass we hoped to catch. As we departed the dock, Dad told Mother to plan dinner for about four p.m., our normal mealtime. How wrong that turned out to be. Circumstances on the water can change at any time.

The Chesapeake Bay is a magnet for commerce, stretching from Pennsylvania south to the Virginia Capes. It is a magnificent body of water that provides access to an abundant and diverse supply of sea life, a transportation route for many types of watercraft, a playground for generations of weekend warriors, and a daily living for working watermen.

On this Saturday, it was our goal to enjoy a day on the water, and with some skill and luck, catch a few rockfish. As we emerged from Solomons' quiet harbor into the Patuxent River, no other boats were visible. This was a sure sign that we needed to proceed approximately two miles to the mouth of the river, where it unites with the Bay at Drum Point Lighthouse.

As we entered the Chesapeake, we noticed a definite increase in wind speed and wave size. It was not the best day to be on the Bay in a small boat with only a twelve-inch freeboard.

Dad piloted the boat north into the wind toward Cove Point Lighthouse, one of the deepest points on the western shoreline, known for large rockfish catches. We each chose a lure we hoped would be a lucky one, added a small piece of pork rind, and strung fifty feet of monofilament across the rocky bottom. The lighthouse point jutting out into the Bay created a breakwater from the waves, a semicalm area in which Dad kept circling.

Making runs up and down the underwater ridge, we boated only one three-pound fish in two hours, so we decided to call it a day. As we reeled in our lines, my father noticed a large cabin cruiser about a quarter mile out in the center of the Bay. Two people on board were waving towels to attract our attention. It's not unusual for people to have trouble out on the water. Generally, they are weekenders, not prepared for a malfunction or knowledgeable about their equipment.

With no other boats in sight, we headed out into the rougher water toward the boat. It was dead in the water and rolling from side to side with each passing wave. As we approached, we observed it to be a yacht about thirty-six feet long with four feet of dead rise. With the wave height now running at three feet, our little runabout was no match for the task at hand.

We maneuvered as close as possible to inquire as to the problem. Their only answer was, "We need a tow."

On the water, there was no option to refuse. We had to attempt a tow in the worst possible conditions. Calling on Dad's experience, I did what I was told and said a little prayer.

We constructed a towrope bridle from anchor rope and attached one end to their bow, and the other end to our engine foundation. Dad was afraid our transom could not take the pounding.

Thus began a treacherous four-mile journey at the rate of one mile per hour, which we weren't sure we would even be able to complete. The towrope was not long enough to keep the yacht from crashing down dangerously close to our small boat each time it crested a large wave. We could not maneuver in close to shore for fear of losing the tow in the shallow surf. There was no additional communication from the yacht as we continued toward Drum Point Lighthouse. Only a seasoned waterman like my father could have accomplished all that he did during the treacherous journey.

Three hours later, we rounded the point and entered the relatively calm waters of the Patuxent River. It was now five-thirty, and with darkness descending, we knew my mother's nerves would be on edge. It was not normal for us to be so late.

Ten minutes later, our luck changed. Two large, familiar island charter boats suddenly appeared, returning after a day's charter. Realizing our situation, the captain of the nearest boat volunteered to take over the tow. We gladly accepted and headed home.

As we entered the harbor at Solomons, we saw an ambulance with red lights bright in the darkened sky sitting at the town marina dock. Dad made mention that someone must have been hurt as we continued up St. John's Creek to our dock.

Thirty minutes later, as we were enjoying a warmed-over dinner, the phone rang. It was the captain of the charter boat that had taken over the tow. He proceeded to tell my father that the owner and captain of the yacht had suffered a heart attack. None of the other three people on board had known what to do or how to run the boat. He went on to say that our actions had saved the man's life. The ambulance and crew we saw at the marina had been waiting for him to arrive so that they could administer aid. The charter boat captain also told my dad that he had given the yacht owner's family my father's name and phone number, and that my father would probably receive some kind of communication from the family for our efforts.

We never heard from the family or learned the fate of the captain, but that didn't make any difference to us. Any time someone is in need on the water, we must do all we can to assist them, simply because to help another in need is the code of the watermen.

DANGER ON THE WATER

When men leave home early in the morning to work on the water, they dress appropriately for the harsh environment they will endure for hours at a time. Men who tong for oysters in the winter usually wear heavy underwear, flannel shirts, bib overalls, and a pair of hip-hugger rubber boots. This attire allows an oysterman to withstand cold wind and rain while he balances himself on the boat's fantail, handling eighteen-foot-long tongs. However, a small slip or a sudden wave can cause him to fall overboard, and if that happens, there is no way for him to get back on the boat. The workboats have no ladders, and once a worker's rubber boots fill with water, as much as two hundred extra pounds are added to his weight This is the fear of every waterman, and it is what caused my dad and his brothers to persuade their father to give up this dangerous trade at age seventy-seven.

One Saturday when I was a teenager, this fear became a reality. On that terrible evening, our next-door neighbor came over to tell my dad that her husband had not returned from a day's work on the river. She asked my father if he could help, in case he'd had engine trouble. My father was close friends with this neighbor and was very familiar with the area he normally worked, and in no time he was in his boat and heading out on the river, not sure what he might find.

Dad spotted the neighbor's boat where he had thought it might be, but as he neared the boat, the scene became clear—a lasting memory that my father never got over. His neighbor and best friend was floating beside his boat, facedown in the water with a rope tied around his wrist. He had fallen into the water and was unable to save himself.

Until the accident, our neighbor's son had followed in his father's footsteps, working full-time on the water. Afterward, he sold his dad's boat and switched to another line of work.

A BOAT WITHOUT A RUDDER

It's August 1960. I have just graduated from the Newport News Apprentice School. After five years of work and study, it's time for a little relaxation. There can be no better way to unwind than spending an afternoon on my dad's new cabin cruiser, so I am headed to my parents' home on Solomons Island.

Steel hull cabin cruiser

The next day is a typical lazy, hazy day of summer. The majestic Patuxent River is smooth as glass, reflecting the white billowing clouds placed as if by hand here and there along the horizon. My dad is eager to show off his new cabin cruiser, recently purchased from a friend. He knows this boat well, having made many minor repairs to it in the past.

As we make our way out into the river, I'm delighted to find that it is exactly the kind of day I was hoping for. We continue out onto the Chesapeake Bay, headed for a location my dad knows will yield an afternoon of fun catching several species of fish.

Dad cuts the engine, allowing the boat to drift with the tide along an underwater ledge. Smaller fish tend to feed along these ledges, sometimes attracting larger fish. I stand at my favorite spot, close to the bow, fishing rod dangling over the side, not sure if I care to be disturbed by a fish on this peaceful, lazy afternoon.

About an hour later, my dad yells that he can hear running water—never a good omen on a boat. He raises a portion of the floorboard to discover six inches of water in the bilge, rising fast. Upon further searching, we determine that the source of the leak is an open hole about two inches in diameter, right where the rudderpost ought to be. There are no other boats in sight—we are on our own. If the flow of water cannot be stopped, we have about thirty minutes before this steel-hulled boat goes under.

Quickly, Dad finds a rag and stuffs it into the hole, using a screwdriver as a ram. Meanwhile, I start the bilge pump and begin to bail out some of the water with a small pail. That's one problem under control —but now we have time to realize that our absent rudder is lying thirty feet under the boat, somewhere on the bottom of the Chesapeake Bay. What to do in a boat with no rudder?

My first thought is to call for help, but Dad calmly starts the engine, looks at me with a smile, and hands me a mop. In his own hand, he holds a broom. He then instructs me to hold on tight—"and when

I tell you, stick the mop into the water." I have used this steering method in my small skiff, using a single oar, but never realized it could be utilized even with a large boat.

With the boat's steering wheel now abandoned, Dad heads the boat into the river toward home. We arrive a little later than we planned, but without any major steering problems. Once again, I marvel at my dad's ability to improvise in any situation.

The incident does not spoil my time at home. It just adds another fond memory to be recalled later, and passed on to my children.

DON'T EAT THE SEAFOOD

The majestic Chesapeake Bay is a natural storehouse of seafood, but in our zeal for a better way of life, we who inhabit the Bay have destroyed—sometimes on purpose, sometimes by accident, and many times through simple carelessness—a large portion of the sea life that once lived there.

For the past two hundred years, the Chesapeake Bay has been slowly dying, a victim in part of the very people who have depended on it the most. The degeneration of the Bay is not part of some grandiose master plan. However, once a natural environment has been altered—no matter the reason—restoration is a slow process that can be accomplished only at tremendous cost, if at all. The Bay has been poisoned by industrial pollutants, farm fertilizers, sewage runoff, and ships' oily discharge, but still it is not a graveyard; it has deteriorated to the point that its sea life is seriously threatened, its marsh grasses have largely been depleted, and its waters are clouded, but still it lives. The water continues to flow freely from the headwaters in central Pennsylvania south through the state of Maryland and into the Atlantic Ocean along Virginia's southeastern coast. In recent years, people living in those states have started a campaign to clean up the Bay, because they know the Chesapeake as more than a body of water—to them, it is a way of life. Depending on their need, the Bay is a highway, a garden, a place to work, or a recreation area—plus a scenic wonderland.

The Bay once teemed with many types of sea life, but today the variety and quality of that sea life is diminished. In studying Virginia history, every schoolchild has read the story of the Native Americans planting a fish under each hill of maize, to be used as fertilizer. When I was a teenager, my grandparents rented small skiffs to tourists who wanted to go fishing around Solomons Island. On warm summer days, a tourist had but to look out over the surrounding waters to locate the fleets of small skiffs that inevitably gathered where fish were being caught.

Today, the types of fish most commonly caught in those days are scarce or nonexistent. Chesapeake Bay oysters, which were once large and plump—the size of your palm—are considerably smaller, and with the size has gone the taste. Limits have been established on the size and quantity of most seafood that today's watermen can harvest. To make matters worse for the watermen, articles in the newspapers proclaim, "DON'T EAT THE SEAFOOD."

I know the Chesapeake Bay, and I know it has a heart, for I have felt its pulse since I was very young. I take strength from the Bay, and I feel at home whenever I'm near its waters. The Chesapeake Bay is on loan to our generation, and it's up to us to pass it along to future generations in better condition than it is in now. We are on the way; the fish are becoming more plentiful, the sea grasses are slowly returning, industrial waste dumping has ceased, and farmers are using protective barriers around their fields to prevent fertilizer runoff. Individual home sewage systems have been modified so that they no longer exit into the Bay and its tributaries, and ship's crews are no longer allowed to dump ship waste or oily bilge water into the Bay. The first steps on a long road back have been taken, and I for one am very glad.

A WATERMAN'S CHRISTMAS

What's a Christmas celebration without a Christmas tree? In our house it had to be a cedar tree, fresh cut to allow the sweet odor to fill all the corners of our small four-room house.

Getting the tree was an event as important as opening presents on Christmas morning. My father, mother, and I would bundle up—Dad with handsaw in place on his belt—and head off the island to a predetermined farmer's woods to find a tree of the proper size and shape. We never made this trip until Christmas Eve, so the tree would be fresh for the entire week of Christmas.

We didn't always agree on which tree to take. My young eyes were looking for the perfect tree, tall and full, while my parents wanted one that would fit in one corner of our living room, mounted on the small platform we used each year for the nativity scene.

Once we arrived home with our prize, Dad would cut away low or broken branches as necessary and mount the tree on the platform. It was left up to Santa to trim—I never saw a decorated tree before Christmas morning. Santa always seemed to decorate the same way, with angel hair covering each bubble light, and strings of green-and-red paper loops running around the tree. Clear plastic icicles dangled from each limb, while here and there a small silver ball could be seen reflecting the lights out into the room. Around the bottom of the tree was a blanket of white spun cotton, which blended with the small white picket fence framing the nativity scene. The edges of the platform were covered with red crepe paper decorated with a brick pattern.

What a sight it was when seen for the first time on Christmas morning! Looking back now, I finally realize the total enjoyment my parents must have gotten in providing that wonderful sight for me each year, at such small expense.

A LIFETIME OF SERVICE

Like me, my younger brother Ronnie did not follow the path to become a waterman. Instead, he quit high school and joined the Army to fight on the front line against the North Koreans. Upon returning to the States, he spent the remainder of his life driving large eighteen-wheel trucks, while volunteering as a fireman and as an emergency medical technician in southern Baltimore. He worked his way up to the position of fire chief.

Ronnie wrote the following poems just before he was laid to rest. My sister-in-law, Edith Robinson, gave me permission to include them, to be printed here for the first time, as a gift to all firemen everywhere.

A Fireman's Prayer
By Ronald Robinson

Lord, I ask myself the reasons why
I have chosen a hobby that people deny.
To volunteer my time to help my fellow man,
to assist and to comfort in any way that I can.
I am laughed at and scorned by people everywhere,
but I continue the job and say a small prayer:
Please, O God, give me the strength that I need
to continue to answer every mournful plea.
To help the homeless, the weak, and the ill.
O God, I pray that these cries will become still.
I pray that all of the suffering that is done
will at last someday be silenced and gone.
But please, Dear Lord, only this I pray,
when my time is near that I can say:
now my time is here, my job is through.
I have done my best, Lord—it is up to you
to place a man in the job I have done
until at last, O God, the job is finally won.

A Fireman's Prayer II
By Ronald Robinson

O Lord, we pray for a quiet day
not another day like yesterday,
when screams and crying could be heard
As fire raced through a burning home,
as children laid upon the ground,
burned so bad without a sound.
As parents grieved for a burned child
and prayed for peace and hope out loud.
Please Lord, let those children live.
Our firemen fought so hard to give
a life of love; don't let it pass.
Give us peace and love that will forever last

Bring peace of mind to our men who fought
a burning fire they thought they lost.
Courageous firemen that through it all
give their hearts and souls to answer the call.
God bless each one of them, O Lord,
and guide them to their just reward.

Painting by author of watermen harvesting oysters from a drag net

About the Author

Sonny Robinson was born on Solomons Island on March 24, 1936, in a small wood frame house close to the ferry dock. He spent his early childhood in Baltimore until the United States became involved with WWII, at which time his family returned to Solomons, where he spent the remainder of his youth. Sonny retired to Florida with his wife, Nancy, in 1995, after forty-two years working for the Newport News shipyard in Virginia. He enjoys boating and fishing.